HEAVEN IS FOR REAL: I DIED APRIL 10TH 1980

The Amazing Story Of A Doctor's Account Of Heaven

Dr. Jim Van Meter

Gbenz Consulting

Heaven Is For Real: I Died April 10th 1980

All Rights Reserved.

Copyright 2015

This book may not be reproduced, transmitted or stored in whole or in part by any means, including graphic, electronic, or mechanical, without the express written consent of the publisher in the case of brief quotations embodied in critical articles and reviews.

Printed In The Unites States Of America

To Larry & Linda

All my love in Christ Jesus,

Hebrews 11:1

Acknowledgement

First of all I would like to thank my Lord Jesus Christ for allowing me to go to Heaven and return back to this earth to be able to share my experience with others. So many people seek and search for answers due to the loss of their loved ones. I pray that this book will help to give them peace,

I would also like to thank my wife of 45 years who has always stood beside me, God gave her to me and she is truly the love of my life. I also want to thank my children who have also stood beside me in good times and bad times.

I would like to acknowledge the death of my dad, mom, sister and my brother-in-law who have died since 1980.

I would like to thanks Kennedy Benedio
CEO www.gbenzconsulting.com
for publishing this book.

Prologue

I was born June 10, 1949;

I died April 10, 1980.

As the doctor and nurses in the operating room were scrambling around to save my life, I remembered thinking **"Someone help me, I'm not breathing here,"** then my heart just stopped. **"What's going on here? Hey guys I'm dying, oh no I'm dead**." I will not see Jan or the Kids again, but that's ok, the Lord will take care of them.

TABLE OF CONTENTS

Acknowledgement

Prologue

The Day of My Death

Heaven Bound

The Time I Could Not See

About the Author

THE DAY OF MY DEATH

"Now faith is the substance of things hoped for, and the evidence of things not yet seen." Hebrews 11:1

Accept me Lord with my child like faith.

Immediately after I died on the operating table in 1980, I remember looking at the doctors and the nurses scrambling around, and one of the nurses made a comment that I was too heavy for her to lift. She was trying to insert the breathing tube down my throat. Dr. Clements took over and said, "**He is a heavy SOB; hurry**, we've lost him." I remember thinking that's odd how could I be outside my body when I am lying right there on the table dead? The doctors and nurses were desperately trying to save my life. They defibrillated me three times, with no response.

It was the spring of 1980 that I learned my father was dying of terminal cancer. The doctors had only given him four to six months to live. It was a devastating time for my mother, my sisters, my brother and I. Dad was the corner stone that held our family together. He was a kind hearted man and was always there for his family and friends. My dad was born in Oklahoma in a small town near the southeastern border of the state; he was the oldest boy of five siblings. He had to quit school in the eighth grade to help support his family during the great depression. He was the kind of dad that other children wished their dad could be like. He taught me at an early age how to hunt and fish safely, and was a master carpenter who also taught me the trade. He could build the finest furniture or build the finest custom home; he could do it all. If a person was in need, he was there to help. He was a God fearing Christian man that taught us by example and not just out of a book. He was a highly respected man at the church and in the community.

I remember when a small church in Carrollton asked my Dad to build a room on to the existing church building; he accepted the job. Later the same day he called a few of his good friends and they completed the add-on in early spring of that year. The church loved their work. To me, that was just my dad being himself. He was just that kind of man that would take charge and get it done. I could not for the life of me figure out why God was taking my dad, when there were so many dads in the world that were terrible fathers and didn't care about their wives or their children. I walked around with the "why me" attitude, not thinking of anyone but me losing my dad; Oh, how I loved my Dad. Sure I loved and adored my wife and children and took care of them, but my mind and heart was worrying about my dad.

My entire life changed on April 10th, 1980. I was training a new sales person for a small chemical company out of Irving, Texas; we sold high end chemicals to industrial manufacturing businesses. My day started out like any other day.

I was up at 7am and gone by 8am. The new representative and I stopped at a fast food place and ate a sausage and egg breakfast, then headed out for our first cold call. Our first call was a box manufacturing company in far North Dallas. I asked to see the maintenance foreman. I asked him about his responsibilities as he talked and showed us all the large equipment that he was responsible for. I made notes on what chemicals he might be interested in. During our conversation with him, he said that all of his men's wives were always complaining about their greasy hands. The men told me that no matter how many times they washed their hands, they weren't able to get them clean. I then took the time to show him a great oil field hand cleaner. After about five men had tried it and were so impressed with how it cleaned their hands, hence I was able to sell him a 55 gallon drum with six free dispensers. What a way to start off the day with a big sale right away.

Next we went to a small city's maintenance department. I had been selling them chemicals for over two years, so I told the representative in training it was up to him to keep the sales' momentum going. I felt good about him, he could talk with anyone; selling should be a natural thing for him. I encouraged him to sell the foreman something he needs and he did, another big sale. Next we made another cold call to a large oil field specialty parts company in North America. I was ready to take the lead again, but the new rep stepped up to make a sale. This was a nice sale, about $300.00 which gave him two sales back to back. He was really after it.

It was now close to lunch and we were down the street from my dad's, so I called him to ask what he and Mom wanted to eat for lunch. My Dad and my Mom both wanted a Mustard Whopper with fries. Steve and I ate a roast beef sandwich with fries from another fast food restaurant. I will never forget the time I spent with my Dad or the meal we ate.

When we got there, I could tell my dad was having a bad day, so I told one joke after another trying to cheer him up. I was trying to not talk about the chemo he was going to get the next day. To see my dad like that broke my heart. Shortly after lunch, I started having stabbing pains in my right side, and it was making me sick to my stomach. I didn't say anything to my dad about it and instead told him that we needed to get back to work. I told him I hated to eat and run, but he knew how that was. When we got back to the car, I asked the trainee rep to drive. He looked puzzled, but took the keys and drove off. I told him what was going on so he took me home. I thought I was going to get sick in the car; by the time I got home, the pain was getting unbearable. He talked nervously the entire way home. When I got home, my wife wasn't there so I paged her. I told the rep that I would be fine and he could leave, as my wife would be home soon. When Jan got home, she knew something was wrong because it was early and

I was lying on the couch. Jan asked me what was wrong and I told her. I thought I was having an appendicitis attack, so she called a doctor who had helped my mother-in-law in the past. The office told her that it would be late before the doctor could see me, and my wife told them that the doctor had to hurry, as it was my appendix. They reluctantly told her to bring me in about 2pm. After checking me, the doctor told me that he felt like it was my appendix and he had my wife take me straight to Memorial Hospital of Garland. They started preparing me for surgery that night; they did not want to wait till' morning, as there was a chance it could rupture. I had eaten lunch, so they had to wait a while before giving me the anesthesia.

It took six hours to line up a surgery room, and seemed like forever before I was taken into surgery. Jan called my parents; she also called my brother and sisters, along with my boss to inform them about what was happening to me. The doctor encouraged us not to worry because I would be in and out in about an hour, and that I would be just fine. The nurse came in and gave me a shot to help me relax, and the next thing I remember was going down the hall and seeing the lights overhead. My wife of 10 years choked back tears and told me she loved me, and I put a thumb up and told her not to worry. As I came into the operating room I saw Dr. Clements all dressed up in his green scrubs. He introduced me to the anesthesiologist. It was then he injected me with something to put me to sleep. He told me to count to 10 but I only made it to 6. I remember thinking, "I just stopped breathing, then my heart stop."

I had a big problem here, because I had just stopped breathing. My heart stopped; I panicked and began to know that I needed someone to help me, then thinking "oh well, I'm dead." I remember thinking that I was going home to be with the Lord and I won't see Jan or the children again on this side of heaven. I felt like it was okay, and they would be fine. I had a good insurance policy and they wouldn't need a thing. But then, I wondered who would teach my son to play ball or walk my daughter down the aisle when she got married.

I thought, "But Lord I have so many things to do. I work hard to take care of my family; I love my family Lord," and then I knew it wasn't about me but the Lord. He had always taken care of my family that He gave me." God would be the one to make sure my son had the talent to play ball and help my daughter to choose the man of her dreams. It has always been about you Lord and I am ready to come home.

"In my Father's house are many mansions: if it were not so I would have told you so. I go to prepare a house for you."

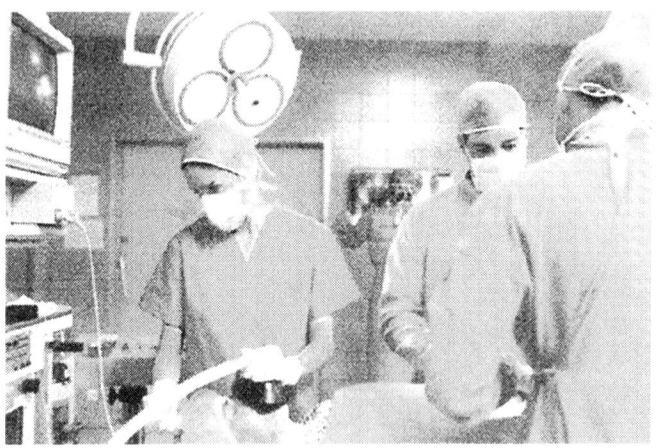

John 14:2

As the doctors and nurses were scrambling around with the crash cart, one of the nurses stated that she was having a hard time lifting me up to insert the breathing tube down my throat. Dr. Clements starting helping the nurse and he said "He is a heavy SOB. Hurry, we are losing him." I remember thinking that it's odd

I am outside of my body looking at my body while they were working on me. The next thing I remember is that someone had put a sign on top of the cabinet that said if you can see this sign wave goodbye.

I did but it was put there as a joke and I felt like this was no joking matter. All of a sudden there was a warm beautiful light that appeared and I was being drawn to it, like a kitten being drawn to a warm bowl of milk. I didn't perceive it as a tunnel but a beautiful light of many colors. It had such a soothing glow in a place filled with darkness all around me. Faster and faster I was being drawn to the light. It seemed so far away but it only took seconds for me to get there. I felt the sensation of flying and it was the greatest feeling I have ever had.

I thought that it must be what an eagle feels like when it is in flight. All of a sudden, I came to an abrupt halt. It felt like an elevator falling from 60 floors high and suddenly stopping at the bottom. Then there was a calmness that came over me like a warm blanket snuggled all around me on a cold winter night. What a beautiful song; where was it coming from? In front of me, behind me, it was from all around me. It was more beautiful than the largest choir I have heard. It came from all around me. They were singing praises to our Lord.

What a calmness came over me; it was like a warm blanket on a cold winter's night; it seemed to just snuggle around me. I knew that nothing on this earth could compare to its beauty. With dark soft green grass, gorgeous flowers, trees and breath taking mountains, I could hear praises being offered up to the Lord. The praises were like sweet honey dripping from a honey comb. There was such heart felt love for Jesus. It made me feel like I wanted to fall to my knees and praise the Lord. There was not just one song, but many of them being offered up at the same time. I could hear them all very clearly. I don't know how that was possible, but it was. If you can imagine the best choir you have ever heard and you multiply that times a million, it would not compare to what I was hearing. Then my attention was focused straight in front of me and I could see a bright light not far ahead of me.

Heaven Is For Real: I Died April 10th 1980

Heaven Bound

As I stared toward the light to the right of me, I saw some of my family that had died before me. My Grandmother, Helen Van Meter, she looked like she was in her early thirty's; she was motioning for me to come over to her. She was such a wonderful Christian and every time we went to see her I would either sit on the front porch or in the living room. She would read and ask us what we thought God was teaching us in His Holy word, the Bible. As I rushed over to see her she said, "You sure do look good Jimmy and I am so glad to see you. You look just like your dad." She threw open her arms to hug me. She is the one that lead me to Christ when I was 10 years old. It was at Bethel Baptist Church in Antlers, Oklahoma during Christmas vacation. I remember giving my life to the Lord that Sunday, and then going over to one of the men's farms and breaking ice on the pond to be baptized. I will never forget when the preacher baptized my uncle L.D. and brought him up out of the water, my dad asked if the water was cold. Uncle L.D. said no, my dad yelled "Dunk him again preacher, he is already lying!" The water was very cold that day but not one of us got sick. When I was 12 years old my grandmother, Helen Van Meter, called my dad and asked if I could go to church summer camp with my cousin Phil Pound, the camp lasted for two weeks. She told my dad that she had already paid for me to go and all he had to do was to bring me to her home in Oklahoma. She told my dad that the church would take me to Balch Springs, Arkansas. It was at that youth camp that I dedicated my life to the ministry. Guy Brisco Van Meter was my grandfather and he was standing beside my grandmother, Helen. He put his arm around me and slapped me on the back and said he was glad to see me. He told my grandmother and I, she was right - I looked like my dad. The one thing that sticks in my mind the most was my loved ones that were burned or broken were whole and looked great. Praise the Lord.

There were family members from both sides of my family; my cousin Larry, who had been killed by a drunk driver when he was 12 years old. He looked so happy and didn't have a scratch on him. Then there was Jimmy, one of my mother's cousins who was killed by a rock crusher, Linda and her two daughters, who were burned to death in a car wreck, all looked young, and were so happy to see me. Linda's two daughters grabbed me and hugged me. I can't even begin to tell you the members of my family who were there. If any of my family members were not there, I didn't know it. I guess that God, in His wisdom, did not want me to remember that. I also remember seeing my friend, Mike. He had given his life to Christ just two weeks before he was killed on a motorcycle. Then there was little Paul. He was a little boy that I found drowned in the lake and was only 8 years old. It was so wonderful to have read that scripture in

Revelation 7:17 that says "…God shall wipe away all tears from their eyes." There were no tears in my family's eyes, praise the Lord. My grandmother called my name and told me that I must go forward to the light.

And to be present with the Lord "2 Corinthians 5:8"

As I approached the light, I knew it was Jesus. His appearance was as bright as the sun, and I could only see an outline of Him, but I could see his eyes they were the most sky blue; I will never forget those eyes. I remembered how Matthew, Mark and Luke all described our Lord's transfiguration on the mountain in front of His inner circle, Peter, James and John. It was the time that His glory showed through Him. I experienced the brilliance of God, His father in Heaven shown through Him. I found it amazing that I talked to Jesus without opening my mouth. I said, "Lord, I am ready to come home now."

When Jesus talked to me, I did not hear Him with my ears but with my soul. His voice was like the waters of the Colorado River running over the rocks; it was so mellow and so relaxing. The words he spoke were not the words I wanted to hear at that time. He said "I'm not ready for you yet, there are things you must do first back on earth," I was in such wonderful place I did not want to go back, "But Lord," I said, "I am ready to come home and I want to stay here with you." I was in such a wonderful place that I didn't want to go back. I repeated what I said "Please Lord let me stay here with you."

Jesus said in a still soft voice "I have many things for you to do, now peace be still and look." I looked and saw the next 40 years or more pass in front of my eyes. Some of the time, there were gaps of time, where I saw nothing. I asked the Lord what was

Missing? But there was only silence. Were those blanks the times where I failed the Lord? I wondered. Were they times that I was not in his perfect will? Was it something bad that happened to me? These are questions that I still have today and I still don't know the answers. It reminds me of the Apostle John who was not to write all he had seen of the end times. Then Jesus said "You must go back now," and with his hand on my forehead he said "Go in peace my child." It seemed like it was only a split second from the time that the Lord had sent me back and I was in the operating room, looking over the doctor's shoulder as he tried to revive me. I watched as he placed the paddles from the defibrillator on me and my body lay motionless. He yelled clear as he shot electrical current through my body and there was no response. He yelled clear again and he shocked me and there was no response. On the third attempt he yelled clear and he shocked me. I felt as if my body sucked me back in the same way I left my body. I left my body and returned to my body through my head. I have seen movies that show the spirit leaving through the middle of the body.

However that was not what I experienced. The next thing I remember was the nurses trying to wake me up. I could sense the concern in their voices, as they said "Mr. Van Meter you have got to wake up now," and "Come on now, wake up." As much as I wanted to wake up, I just could not do it. I could not move any part of my body. I felt the sensation that I was moving as they rolled me down the hall to Intensive Care. When we arrived there the nurse gave some report to the CCU physician. I heard him say to put me in room 3. When the nurse came to take my vitals she checked to see if my eyes were rolled up to the top of my eye socket; a person in a coma does this. They were still rolled back and would remain that way for hours. The anesthesiologist told my wife that they were having problems waking me up from the anesthesia and asked if I had ever had that problem before. She told them that they had a small problem waking me up when I had my knee surgery in Germany, but that it didn't really take that long. What they told my wife was not what she found when she walked in my room in the intensive care unit. I was in a coma and they did not know if I was going to make it or not.

They told her that we would have to wait to see if I was able to wake up and come out of the coma. All during the night as nurses and friends came in to see me, I knew what time it was because I could hear them talking about it. At about midnight my boss and his wife came into the room to check on me. Larry and Phyllis had been friends for several years.

Larry came over to the bed and said "Wake up Jim; it's time to go to work." They talked nervously in the room and Larry kept poking me from time to time trying to get some response from me but to no avail. The nurse came in several times during the night to check the position of my eyeballs and to see if they were in the center yet; the sign that I was out of the coma. It was around 3am while my wife, my mom and dad were in the room, that the doctor told them that the longer I was in a coma the more difficult it would be for me to come out of it. The doctor recommended that they call other family members and tell them to come to see me just in case. My dad asked the doctor if I was not going to make it, the doctor said, "I just don't know but I am hopeful that he might respond to one of them." My wife, Jan asked the doctor what had happened to me; he told her that they didn't know, but they were doing some tests. He also told my family that they might want to pray but they told him that they already were.

At about 5:00 in the morning, the nurse came in to check my vitals and raised my eyelids again and even called my name but nothing happened. Then the nurse slapped my face and said "Wake up." She raised my eyelids and I was looking straight at her. She called the doctor in and told him that I was waking up and he came into my room. He lifted my eyelids and told me that if I could hear him move my eyes. I moved my eyes rapidly and he told me I could slow down that I was going to be fine. He told me that he would come back in a little while to see if I could get off of the ventilator. The next 2 hours were strange to say the least. Within 30 minutes, I could feel a warm sensation coming down from my forehead and as it passed my eyes, I was able to open them. As it passed my face I could move my nose and my chin. It was just like when your hand goes to sleep and you can't move it until the blood flow comes back into your hand. That is the way it was affecting my entire body. It was about another 30 minutes before the warmth got to my hands and I could move them. At that time I motioned for my wife to give me a pen and paper and I wrote in a circle, "Get this thing out of my mouth because it is hurting me." It took at least an hour before I was able to move my entire body. The doctor finally came in at 8am and said he was going to try to remove the tube from my throat. He told me not to worry, that first he was going to open a venting tube to see if I could breathe on my own first. As he opened the vent he could tell that I could not breathe. The doctor told me to try to take a deep breath and I did.

I was finally able to breathe on my own. That was the greatest feeling here on earth. Words can't describe that feeling. The doctor removed the breathing tube and I was on my way to recovery. What I didn't realize was that I had lost some of my memory of some of the people and events that happened the year before. Doctor Clements came into the room later that afternoon to talk with me. He told me they were running tests to determine why my body shut down the way it did. He told me that I was a very lucky man to even be alive. I told him that luck didn't have anything to do with it. I told him that it was God's will that I was still alive. I then began to tell him about my near death experience. He stopped me to explain that when the blood is cut off from the brain a person will begin to hallucinate. I asked him why he called me a heavy SOB then. He said "We were losing you and I was trying to save your life." I asked him if my body was shut down and I was hallucinating how would I know what you said? He looked puzzled but then smiled and said "If you were out of your body tell me what you saw", I asked: "Like what the sign on the locker that said if you see this wave good bye."

He got up and left the room. About an hour went by and he came back in. His jaw almost hit the ground as the old saying goes. He said "Let's start over and tell me everything that happened." I went on to tell him everything in detail and he spent over an hour writing down the things I told him. Before I left the hospital the doctor came into my room to explain what had happened to me. They gave me Anectine, and my body had no cholinesterase inhibitors to metabolize the Anectine. I have a tag with that information on it that I carry with me to make sure that no doctor gives me that medication again.

THE TIME I COULD NOT SEE

It has been decades since my near death experience and I have seen the years that were in the future that Christ had showed me. During that time, I noticed that there were events that he did not show me. They were blacked out. Today as I look back I can honestly say that some of the events were: the death of my Dad James Daniel Van Meter in January 1981, the death of my mom, Hazel Virginia (Spain) Van Meter, the death of my dear cousin Angie Seale in 2000 and her dad my Uncle Charles Seale in 2001. There was also the death of my grandmother Minnie Lee (Lee) Spain, my brother in law Gary Lynn Graham,

the 911 terrorists' attack on the World Trade Center in New York; the death of my little sister Deborah Ann (van Meter) Graham in November 0f 2014. These were just some of the things Jesus did not let me see in the future.

ABOUT THE AUTHOR

Jim Van Meter was born June 10,1949. He attended Carrollton elementary, Dewitt Perry Junior High, and RL Turner High School He attended Dallas Baptist University for a year prior to enlisting into the US Army. He is a decorated war veteran. Jim received a Doctorate in Alphabiotics in 1991 and a Doctorate in Divinity in 1993. Jim is a traditional Naturopath; he received his training and his degree from Trinity School of Natural

Health in 1996. He also received his Masters of Herbology from Trinity. Jim, and the entire staff are Licensed as Doctors of Pastoral Services. He received his License from the PMA in 2010. As the senior pastor I know we cannot heal or cure anyone and that is why we pray for each person that comes here, that God will heal them.

Bio-feedback

The L.I.F.E. System identifies and records subtle, informational "stress potentials" provided by the client through the 5 point harness system. The computer evaluates these responses and then challenges the individual with the information by feeding it back to them. Not only does this machine provide valuable, specific information, but it also aids in the stimulation of the body's own healing systems.

ES Teck

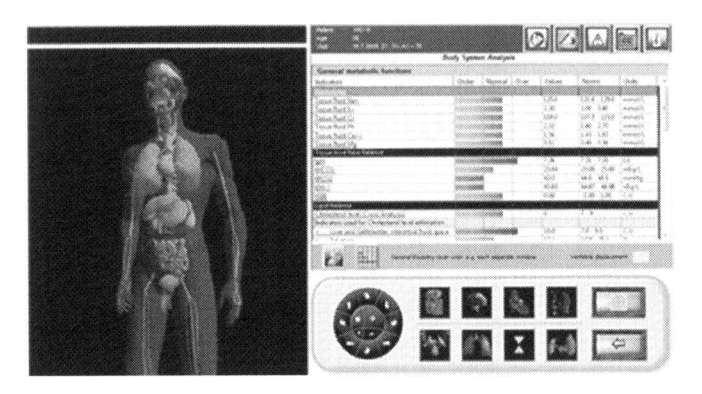

The ES Teck is a full body scanning device. It is non-invasive and yet provides an accurate assessment of a person's physiology. It gives a visual view of the health and stress level of organs, the autonomic nervous system and heart rate variability in just minutes!

Services Offered:

Our signature service is the full body scan, which includes comprehensive testing on the L.I.F.E system biofeedback machine AND on the ES Teck machine. These machines give very specific information that is specific to the client.

- Biofeedback (L.I.F.E. System)
- Es Teck Full Body Scan
- Thermography
- Interactive Metronome Therapy
- Lymph Therapy/Drainage (ST8)
- Far-Infrared Sauna
- Alphabiotic Alignments
- Custom Homeopathic & Herbal Remedies
- Detoxifying Ionic Foot Soak
- Natural Hormone Replacement

- 21 Day Detox Program
- Allergy and Hormone Testing
- Whole Body Vibration (weight loss)
- Massage Therapy

North Texas Wellness Center

At the North Texas Wellness Center we believe in a preventative, holistic approach. We are a complete holistic health care clinic that offers the most updated technology and care that is individualized and personal.

Naturopath David Van Meter, CNHP
Naturopath Jim Van Meter, DA, DD
Naturopath Jan Van Meter ADN, MH, BS

4011 W Plano Pkwy Suite 130 Plano, TX 75093

North Texas Wellness Center
We believe in a holistic, individualized

approach to health. We pair traditional naturopathy with the most updated technology to facilitate optimal wellness.

Far Infrared Sauna

Infrared heat rays warm your body directly, allowing deep penetrating heat at a more pleasant temp of 100IF-150FF. The health benefits include: burning 600 calories/30 min, pain relief, detoxification of organs through sweat, improve skin complexion, improve circulation and cardiovascular health, increase energy, speed recovery from injury, and increase immune system function.

Interactive Metronome

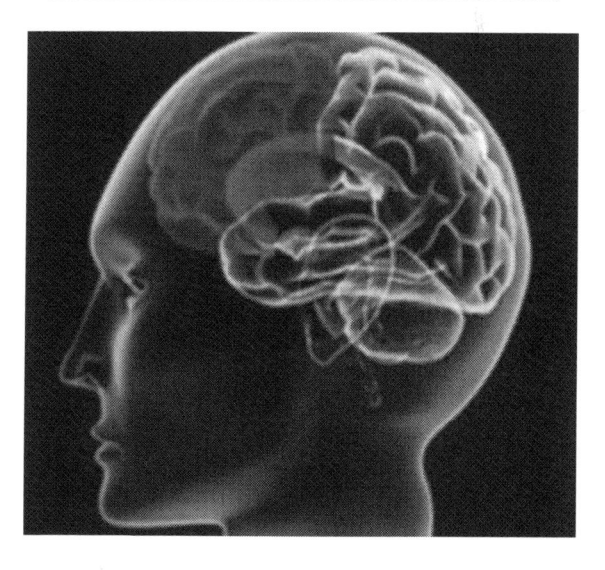

The Interactive Metronome (IM) is a research-based training program that helps children and adults overcome attention, memory, and coordination limitations. IM works for people of all ages who have a variety of conditions affecting their cognitive and physical abilities. Whether you are pursuing outcomes in focus, self-control, speech/language, reading, coordination, or gait/balance, IM is the tool that helps you address the core deficit in timing while customizing exercises, engaging the brain, and pushing your patient to achieve maximum success.

Ion Foot Detox

The Ion Foot detox is a remarkable way to detoxify your body. Your feet are the medium through which negatively charged ions pass into your body. Once inside these charged ions attract toxins and carry them back out through your feet. This is one of the easiest ways to quickly detoxify your body.

__Thermography__

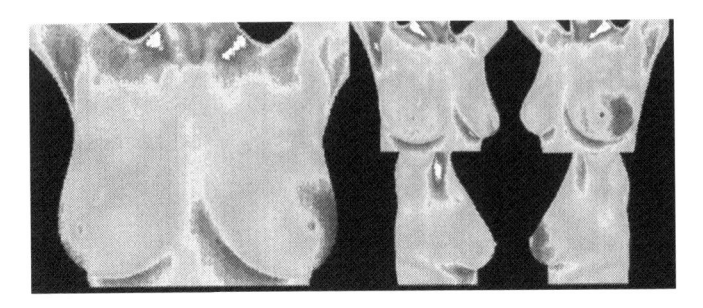

Surpassing other screenings in safety and detection, thermography is the new go-to for preventative breast screening. The-rmography is able to pick up on areas of concern years before other assessment tools. Another major benefit to thermographic imaging is that you don't expose yourself to the harmful radiation in x-rays/mammograms. Every woman should get a regular thermography!

Maximizing Your Marketing & Business Success

www.GbenzConsulting.com

We have a host of Services:
Digital Marketing/ SEO Get Clients/Patients for your Business Get Business Credit Book Publishing

Coaching Services: Maximizing Your Marketing & Business Success Life/Business Coaching Wellness Coaching

We have served many Happy Clients and You are Next!

Have you Heard About "Miracle Water?"

We have technology that produces a type of water that took a Stage 4 Cancer person working with Hospice and about to die in 2009 to Healthy now in 2015. He is still Living and Going Strong!!!

Go here
http://www.KangenWaterIsGood.com

Call Today **(214) 494-9551** for a Complimentary Consultation.

As Seen On: abc NBC CBS FOX CNN

Made in the USA
San Bernardino, CA
10 October 2015